The Art of Self Massage

The DIY Guide For Your Own Tension and Trigger Points

Dr Jason Cain PT, DPT

Disclaimer

Photography by Robert Barlow

Permission for use of Thera Cane® (a product by Thera Cane Company) and RangeRoller™ (a product by Medi-Dyne) has been obtained. I have no affiliation with either product, I just happen to like them. I purchased both years ago on my own. If there is some other product that you know of that works better let me know.

Copyright 2019 Jason Cain

ISBN: 9781099943706

Dedication

Thank you to all the friends and family who have helped with the creation of this book. And for their understanding and patience. I couldn't have done it without you!

TABLE OF CONTENTS

1 SECTION: THE ART OF MASSAGING

1.1 INTRODUCTION

First off let me explain the purpose to writing this book. As a practicing physical therapist for the past 12 years, patients have constantly stated they wished they had learned some of the techniques that I have educated them about self massaging a long time ago.

The intent and design of this book is to aid you in taking better care and control of your body and improve your knowledge of how to manage your pain and limitations. By pinpointing and treating your own trigger points with the use of inexpensive items, even those that can be found around the house, I hope to impart upon you ways to alleviate these tightnesses and make the knots/trigger points disappear.

The information provided does not take the place of common sense and should not go against the advice of your own medical professional.

WHAT IS A KNOT OR TRIGGER POINT?

So what is a knot or trigger point. There are many ideas and theories as to what a knot or trigger point are, but in essence they are the same thing. The simplest answer is that they are areas within your muscles that when palpated (felt through the skin), you feel a nodule, small bump or just plain tightness within the muscle.

A word of caution: There are other things in the body that can feel lumpy. If you are unsure as to what you are feeling go ask your medical professional.

1.2.1 Why are you tight in the first place: Weakness, Injury, Overuse, Posture

If weakness is an issue, your body will compensate and joints will be unstable or used improperly. You will continue to have persistent tightening/retightening of areas. Start by seeking advice from a physical therapist to aid in rebalancing your strength and improved overall posture. Of if you are an avid reader, I will have another book about strengthening soon to be released.

When a body part is injured, the surrounding areas will tighten in order to help preserve and protect the injury, preventing further damage. In this instance, you need to make sure the area appropriately heals before massaging it. Many of us tend to take medications for pain or inflammation. However, when we do this we become less aware of our pain, which opens us up for more injury. You need to remember that pain is our bodies way of telling us to be careful and not do too much. As you heal the body will begin to loosen up, or you can start to gently use some of the techniques that will be discussed in this book.

Overuse and posture go hand-in-hand. If you have poor posture, the muscles will be working harder in order to help maintain your current poor posture. Overuse also occurs when you end up just doing too much, whether from a new exercise or just living life.

Let us say you work a normal 8-5 job Monday to Friday and do not spend a substantial amount of time on weekdays exercising or in motion. The weekend comes around and you decide to do all the housework, cut the lawn, rake the leaves, and then go for a 20 mile bike ride. Well guess what, your body is not conditioned do go from one extreme (constant rest) to another (constant work).

Just to give you more perspective, a week contains 168 hours. How many of those hours are spent sitting or laying down vs being upright and moving around? If you are like most of the people I see, you sleep, sit to eat, drive to work, sit at work (get up a few times for things, but really this is almost negligible), eat lunch at your desk, work some more, drive home, sit to eat dinner, sit and read/watch TV, then go to bed. And just for a side thought, I do not consider standing in one place while working on a computer to be much of a step above sitting, it may be better than sitting, but I think that can be up to debate as to how much better it truly is.

There are fleeting moments in the day spent moving around, so to spend most of ones time with non-movement during the week then expect the body to handle a large workload on the weekend is not realistic. We need to manage our bodies better to help prevent overuse injuries. When we are younger we can tend to brush off the effects of overuse because we heal more quickly, but as we age, the effects of overuse become much more noticeable.

As I mentioned before, posture is a type of overuse, but a "much more easily" correctable one. I use the quotes because even though we can tell ourselves to fix our posture, we tend to constantly forget about using proper posture. How many times did your mother say, "sit up straight" or "stop slouching." Similar to the "don't make that face or it will get stuck that way," your body will actually get stuck that way if you keep a constant poor posture.

I have noticed that over the years, teenage posture has gotten worse and worse. I would propose the simple rational reason is most likely the small electronic devices that have become permanently implanted into their hands that causes them to look down for massively extended time frames. The long-term ingrained habit combined with the use of laptops and other computing devices further cements poor posture that will take a great deal of effort to correct. External reminders and proper strengthening will help to improve the posture, and just trying to be more self-aware of how you are positioning yourself (right now I am grabbing a pillow to prop my computer higher on my lap as I realize I am not following my own advice, see how easy it is to fall into the traps of poor posture).

So to sum it up, if we can manage to overcome our weaknesses, be more careful when injured, be mindful of what we can actually manage (not overuse our bodies), and have better posture we can help to decrease the trigger points, knots, areas of tension that are plaguing our bodies. So read further to begin to understand how to have better control over yourself.

1.3 TOOLS OF THE TRADE:

The main tools that you will want to find or purchase are listed below. They come in three main shapes: spherical, cylindrical, and other. A brief word on each will follow. As each body part is talked about advantages and disadvantages will be listed for specific items.

1.3.1 Spherical Objects

Tennis ball:

One of the easiest items with which to massage yourself. Very versatile to use as you will soon find out. It can be used either full size or cut in half (explained later on). I have not found that one brand is better than another, if anyone feels differently, please email me and let me know.

Figure 1: Tennis ball, varying level of being cut

*NOTE: when cutting a tennis ball in half please be careful as the ball tends to want to roll away, leaving you open to stabbing yourself. I have found that a PVC pipe cutter works very well if you plan on cutting many tennis balls.

Lacrosse ball:

Works the same as the tennis ball, but is harder and can penetrate deeper.

Golf ball:

Even deeper than the lacrosse ball. Works great on the feet, especially when frozen.

Other spherical objects:

There are many things that are round and you can massage with (for purchase or free). Be creative the world is more than happy to help you. There are types of balls sold specifically for massaging that have spikes. I find that these are not meant for deeper work as the skin tends to get aggravated. The spikes work best when working more gently.

1.3.2 Cylindrical Objects

Rolling pin

Not just for baking anymore. The handles make it easier to use and maneuver. It is really too hard to be lay upon it, so do not try.

Massage stick

Similar to a rolling pin but with fancy knobs or discs on it to help penetrate the muscle deeper than a rolling pin could go. The RangeRoller™ is an example of a massage stick that I personally like due to the varying levels of thickness of the discs. Other options can be purchased at a local store or online vendor used.

Figure 2: RangeRoller™, one brand of hand rollers. See the varying thickness of the discs

Can of soup

Meant to be used by hand for rolling the thighs if you do not have a massage rolling stick or rolling pin. I guess it could also be used for the forearms or calves too, otherwise attempting to lay on it is not advisable.

Frozen bottle of water

Meant for the foot. Place it on the ground and enjoy (read the foot section further for full details).

Foam roller

The epitome of cylinders. It is not just for athletes, if you like to go for a walk on a regular basis, the foam roller can be one of your best friends. They come in different densities (how hard it is) as well as with ridges. I personally do not feel as though the ridges make much of a difference other than being more sensitive to the skin, but everyone has different tastes. The color of the roller does not make a difference, so pick the one you like or that is the cheapest.

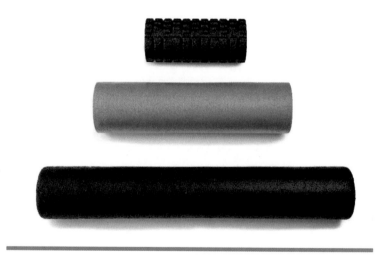

Figure 3: Varying foam roller sizes

1.3.3 Other

Vibrating massagers

You see these in the stores all the time. Some people think they feel great, others think they feel weird. You just have to try one and make your own decision. Hey, they even make whole chairs that vibrate and massage. A consideration to keep in mind is that certain intensities of vibration will actually excite a muscle and cause it to tighten further rather than relaxing it, just be careful with the settings. Also make sure before purchasing an item how you will actually reach the body part you want to massage. Let us say that if you want to massage your upper back and you buy a small handheld device, it could be very awkward to actually reach without straining one of your shoulders (which would defeat the purpose of massaging in the first place).

Curved sticks or canes

This can be as simple as taking an actual cane handle or purchasing a special device such as the Thera Cane®. I personally like the Thera Cane® as it is easy to use and can hit many hard to reach places while sitting in the comfort of your home. As the balls and cylinders usually require you to be lying or standing, with the Thera Cane® you are able to relax and sit. The curve of the stick facilitates reaching the upper traps and the quadratus lumborum (QL) muscles much more effectively than with almost any other device.

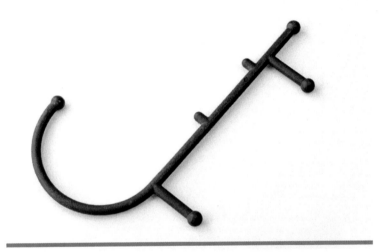

Figure 4: Thera Cane®, the hooked portion allows for better penetration of those hard to reach areas.

1.3.4 Just Plain Other

There are many things in the world to use. Bears rub on trees all the time! Just make sure whatever you are rubbing against is stable and stationary.

1.4 PRINCIPLES OF MASSAGE

1.4.1 Basics

If you have a firm understanding of massaging and what you should be feeling in your body, then feel free to skip to the next chapter. If not, then please continue in this section as you will learn the basics of how to apply appropriate pressure to avoid hurting yourself.

Do not kill yourself. The old adage of "no pain, no gain" is a terrible one to follow. Often misunderstood, pain is your body's way of telling you:

1) stop what you are doing

2) assess the situation to determine if it is something you are doing wrong

3) make the necessary adaptations so that the pain stops

When applying self massage, I recommend to my patients to keep it comfortable. When massaging, say to yourself one of 4 things:

1) "Wow this feels good"

2) "This hurts, BUT it feels good"

3) "This just hurts"

4) "I don't think I'm doing anything"

Some people have the idea there is a choice 5) "This feels good, but it isn't doing anything." I disagree, if it feels good, it generally means that you are having success with the massaging. You are always at liberty to apply more pressure. But a word of caution, I give the analogy of applying salt to food. Add a little bit at a time and see the results. If you add too much all at once then you cannot really take it away, especially when it comes to the body. If you do too much you can irritate an area, and then need to let it calm down before continuing.

Basically, if you want to clench your teeth, ball your fists, or curl your toes; you are pushing too hard. To get the maximum benefit, you MUST focus on relaxing while you are working on yourself. A perfect example of why you must relax can be seen in the figure 5 and 6. If you look closely at the calf in figure 5 you will notice that when the foot is pulled upward and tension/stretching is placed on the calf the foam roller is not sinking in as deeply as when the foot is relaxed in figure 6. Relaxing will allow you to get deeper into the muscle.

Be especially careful when working around the spine and near the rib attachments. The risk of injuries is greater in these areas as are some other key points that we will talk about in the coming section. I will reiterate these points again and again; as repetition is the key to actually learning and creating new habits.

A massage from another is almost always better than one you can do yourself. If nothing else that human touch makes a world of difference. So, if you have a friend or loved one that you can convince, see if they will swap you a massage or maybe you can do an extra chore/job for them.

Figure 5-6: On the Top figure the foot is pulled up putting tension in the calf. In the figure below it the foot is relaxed downward allowing the foam roller to penetrate deeper into the calf

If you either have friends who are massage stingy, not very good at it, or you would just rather not have someone else touch you, then this book is just right for you.

1.4.2 Now How Do I Help Myself Without Hurting Myself

When selecting a massage apparatus, first think about the size of the muscle you are actually trying to treat. What you might notice from the list above is that the objects are either spherical or cylindrical. If you are trying to get into a smaller more specific area, then a spherical object is your best bet. If you are trying to be general or target a larger area of treatment, then something more cylindrical is appropriate.

For the ease of reading, hereafter I will refer to the spherical objects as tennis balls and the cylindrical objects as foam rollers. These two will be your most common apparatus of choice.

The hardness of the object will dictate the aggressiveness of the massaging. Something softer will tend to be more comfortable; while harder objects are more intense and will get deeper into the tissue. Again, you have to keep focusing on how good/bad the pressure feels, i.e., if it hurts and DOES NOT feel good, then you must lighten up or stop. It is not uncommon for one area to need more aggressive treatment as compared to another. Do not be shy about using less pressure. You are not a wimp. You are only starting to become more in tune with your body.

There is not a specific direction of force that needs to be applied. The most important part is to listen to the body. As can be seen in figure 7 on the next page, there are various options for the direction of force to be applied: force being applied in long strokes up and down; strokes at an angle; and lastly there is no moving back and forth, only rocking side to side (as shown by the arc). Make your own combination of movements and find what works for you. Each area of the body likes different things. In the following sections I have tried to lay out the basic and most common methods that can be used. Feel free to be inspired and try new things, just remember "IT MUST FEEL GOOD!"

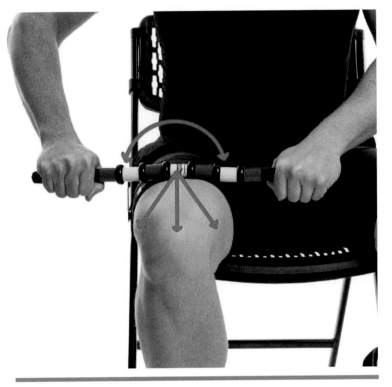

1.4.3 The Wall, the Floor, or the Hand?

This section covers how to apply pressure to your trigger point. The main options are laying on the floor, leaning against the wall, or using your hands. If you are truly lucky you may be able to find someone else that is willing to apply the pressure for you.

Figure 7: Example of working in different directions with the RangeRoller™. Play with it and see how it feels.

In essence, use of your hands applies the least amount of force. It also provides a challenge to relaxing while applying force; and can be the most tiring. However, you can be more fine-tuned to finding spots with your hands than the other options. You can either apply the pressure with your hand itself or with one of the aforementioned implements.

Next, we have the wall which provides greater force than the hands alone, but not maximum force. The wall is notably advantageous for the hips and higher areas of the body. The major advantage of the wall is the ability to adjust your pressure, especially for sensitive areas. If you are applying too much force then scoot your feet closer to the wall, allowing you to lean less, decreasing the pressure. If you need further force move your feet farther away from the wall to allow you to lean harder against the wall applying deeper force. By adjusting where your feet are placed you have increased control using the wall than when using the floor. Remember that relaxing gives you the best results.

Note: When using a tennis ball for treatment of the rib cage and near the spine, I always recommend using the wall as opposed to the floor. I feel that these areas are more susceptible to damage due to the control issues while on the floor.

Lastly, rolling on the floor allows you the maximum force to be applied while reducing the amount of control. In general, the foam roller is the way to go when self massaging an area on the floor. Once again, you must relax in order to get the most benefit from self massaging. The more you are lifting yourself off of the object then the less you are relaxing resulting in wasted efforts and time.

In the following sections I will discuss the different positions in order to allow appropriate form and maximum relaxation with each of the different objects of massage

1.4.4 How Long Do I have to Do This?

Timing is important while massaging. Frequently I see people at the gym rolling themselves for 30 seconds over and area and calling it quits. This will do almost nothing for you. You must perform the massage techniques that are to follow for a minimum of one minute over an area to have an effect. I generally recommend 2-5 minutes of work on an area before moving on to another or ceasing a massage session.

Sometimes you find a good stop that you just want to lay into, this can be very effective if you do not stay locked into the spot for too long. My definition of too long is more than 90 seconds without moving; if you are applying sufficient force, staying locked in for more than 90 seconds can have potential negative results due to reduce the blood flow into the muscles which would potentially cause damage.

1.4.5 Precautions and Contraindications

Contraindications (just don't do it):

Never try to massage an area that has swelling. You could end up causing extra damage or further swelling.

Never massage over an open wound.

Over a bruise.

Over a broken bone.

Please use common sense, as stated earlier, IF IT JUST HURTS, DON'T DO IT.

Precautions:

Be careful of tendons and ligaments. For the purposes of this book we are focusing on muscles. Leave the fascia, ligaments, and tendons to the professionals, so that extra trauma does not occur. Going forward, keep in mind that this book is talking about how we will handle the different muscle groups throughout the body.

If it hurts, EASE OFF (It is amazing how many times I have to say this, but yes, it is actually necessary).

If you find any of the following, you should possibly have an evaluation by one of your local healthcare providers to help determine what is the cause of your tightness, as massaging alone will not be your answer:

1) that you are working an area over and over again without finding relief

2) that you keep tightening back up despite having not changed your activity level

3) it hurts regardless of the pressure you are applying

Persistent tightness indicates an underlying issue. If you achieve consistency with working on tightened areas then you should notice that the tissue becomes looser and looser with less restrictions.

Warning

Again, the information provided does not take the place of common sense and should not go against the advice of your own medical professional. The following sections are now the specific instructions for each body region.

2 SECTION: PARTS OF THE BODY

2.1 HEAD/JAW

We chew, we talk, we chew some more, then we clench our teeth when stressed. The jaw gets used and neglected and sometimes used as a head rest. There are four main muscles that open and close the jaw. We will be addressing two of these muscles below as the other two muscles are not easily accessible.

2.1.1 Masseter

Pressure can be applied with the fingertips. Work this area gently as there are glands nearby that do not want to be pressed. Start at the base of the jaw near the backside and apply a gentle pressure inward. You can work the hands upward the cheek bone as seen in figure 8, staying near the backside of the jaw. I generally recommend using both hands at the same time in order to not push the jaw out of alignment.

2.1.2 Temporalis

Pressure can be applied with either the fingertips or the

Figure 8: Using the fingertips, apply a gentle pressure

heel of the hand. Use whichever is more comfortable. The muscle fans from the temple to almost the backside of the head. You will have to press closer to the front of the head as seen in figure 9 and then towards the back of the head as seen in figure 10. As you apply a gentle pressure in toward the head you can then lift the hands slightly toward the ceiling to semi stretch the muscle. You can also apply circular or front/back motions for a varied effect. You must use both hands at once as to not strain the neck; the pressure must be equal. Additional techniques are detailed in figures 11 and 12.

Figure 9-10: Temporalis release show above with heel of the hand to the back portion. The figure below shows heel of the hand to the mid/front portion

Figure 11-12: Temporalis release shown above with fingertips to the mid portion. The figure below shows force applied with heel of the hands, elbows out to the side generally allows for more pressure to be applied

2.2 NECK

2.2.1 Sub Occipital (base of the skull) and Neck

For neck pain or headaches, I generally recommend laying on your back and placing 2 full tennis balls or 2 half-cut tennis balls under the neck or base of the skull as seen in figure 14 on the next page. The use of the half-cut tennis ball will reduce the pressure on the neck making for a more gentle massage. There does not need to be any motion here while working, just lay and relax over the ball; you can gently turn the head side to side if you wish, but keep it a small motion. One tennis ball can be used, but I feel that unless you are very heavily muscled, you can run the risk of knocking a vertebrae out of alignment or being too aggressive to the spine in general.

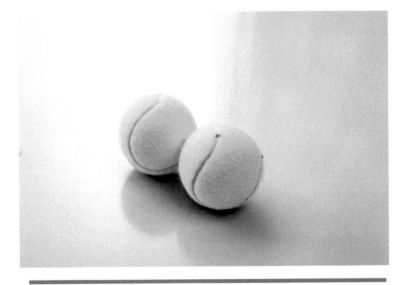

Figure: 13: Two tennis balls for massaging the back of the neck/head.

Note: You find that the tennis balls keep escaping if they are not tethered together in some manner. Place them in a sock and tie off the end or tape the balls together. Before taping them try and figure out how far apart you want them to get your favorite spot, they may not have to be perfectly touching each other to be effective.

Figure: 14: Two tennis balls, relax and breathe deeply as the balls do their work

2.2.2 Upper Trap and Levator

The majority of people carry their stress here. It is one of the tightest area of the body and one of the most awkward places to reach with a tennis ball. A cane or curved stick actually works much better here. As you can see in the figures below (15, 16, and 17) by using the curved portion of the Thera Cane® you are able to apply ample force to the upper trap and gently massage away with minimal stress and work for the arms.

Depending on the length of your arms, you will have to play with hand positioning while using the Thera Cane®. As you practice more you will get a better feel for how to apply the pressure. To keep the Thera Cane® from sliding you want to gently press downward and then pull forward; this will catch the upper trap in place helping to release the muscle.

Figure 15: Thera Cane®, front/angled view to see hand positioning

On the next page, in figure 18, you will see the Thera Cane® moved to the corner of the shoulder blade to refocus the pressure onto the levator.

Figure 16-17: Thera Cane®, Top figure shows an angled/side view, while the lower figure shows pushing downward and forward on the upper trap

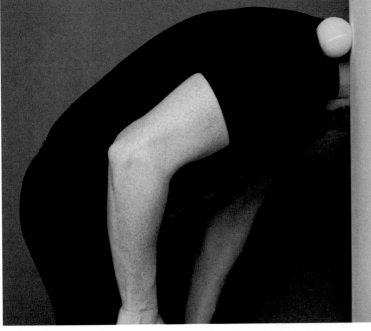

For those without a massage stick (which can be inexpensively purchased online), use a tennis ball (pictured below in figure 19). It works best against either a door frame or a corner. Start by leaning forward and holding the tennis ball up by the side of the neck you want to treat (use the opposite hand to hold and maneuver the ball, so that it does not escape and you crash into the wall). There really is not much room to be able to move here, depending on your size you just have to play with it and see what works. The tennis ball being placed into pillowcase can help reduce frustrations if you keep dropping the ball, at least it will not roll as far away.

Figure 18-19: Thera Cane® shown in the top figure has been moved to the corner of the shoulder blade to refocus more on the levator. Tennis ball shown in the lower figure to the upper trap. Place the ball and lean forward. You may need to keep your other hand on the ball to prevent it from escaping

2.2.3 Scalene

Located at the side/front of the neck, the scalene tends to be over tightened due to poor posture. Because of the precarious position of this muscle and important vessels underneath of it, I generally do not recommend use of a tool here, just use the hand. You will place the fingertips just above the collar bone and curl the fingers gently down. At the same time you can gently tilt the head to the side (away from the fingers) and look slightly upward which will give you a stretch of the muscle. Make sure that you do not get any pinching or pain in the neck on either side, if you do, STOP. Also, if you get any tingling into the arm or hand, STOP. If you are getting pain, you may need to seek your local physical therapist for further assessment and assistance.

Figure 20: Using the hand, gently grasp just above the collar bone, for a further stretch tilt the head to the side and look upward

2.3 CHEST/SHOULDER

2.3.1 Pecs

The pectoralis (pec) muscles need work because if they are too tight, it will be more difficult to obtain a good posture or easily squeeze your shoulder blades together. Also, if you are having shoulder pain, tightness in the pecs can limit the proper motions in the shoulder. The tennis ball is your best bet here. The foam roller can also be used, but is just plain awkward if used directly.

To use the foam roller, you will position yourself on top of the roller as seen below in figure 21 and 22. Rolling is very awkward and it is easier to just leave the roller in one spot and kind of rock on it gently rather than trying to roll. Proceed further for the tennis ball which is more effective.

Figure 21 and 22: Foam roller to the pec, angled view, as well as a top view

Bonus: For a nice stretch of the pec, you can use the foam roller as listed below. Laying on your back with the head supported on the roller. Unless you are very tall, your tailbone should be nicely supported as well. Lay with your arms out to your side and relax and breath. For an extra stretch of the pecs and to open up the chest and ribs more, you can gently swing your arms upward/downward like you are making a "snow angel," as seen in figure 23, 24, and 25.

Figure 23-25: Foam roller "snow angel." Top Left figure shows starting position with the arms at the side. You will then flip the palms upward and start moving the arms up and out to the side as shown in the Middle figure, working towards raising your arms over your head into the finished position as seen in Bottom Right figure.

To use a tennis ball an outward corner or a door frame work best. With the door frame you can really only go up/down because of the nature of the frame. The corner allows for multiple directions, such as up/down, side/side, or circular. There again, the farther your feet are from the vertical surface the more aggressive, the closer they are in the less pressure you will apply.

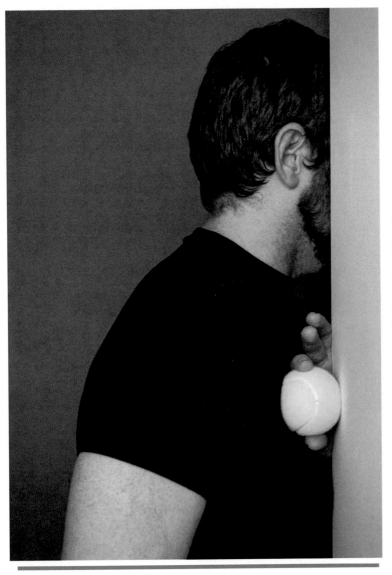

Note: Make sure you keep the hand of the arm you are not treating close around the ball, so that it does not escape and you end up slamming your shoulder against the wall.

Figure 26: Tennis ball against wall, the best pressure you can get for the pec.

The Thera Cane® works well in terms of getting a good release of the pec. Pick one of the rounded ends and poke away. The cane gives you better leverage than using your hand alone, but still puts work on the opposite arm.

Figure 27: Thera Cane®, using one of the points to release the pec. Better than hand alone

If you cannot find a wall or any other piece of equipment, then you always have your other hand to be able to apply the pressure. Be warned though, the downside to using your hand is that it tires the fingers plus has the chance of tightening the opposite pec (which can be counterproductive if you keep switching back and forth between each side.

Figure 28: Pressing with the hand may be the least effective, but it is better than nothing.

2.3.2 Rhomboids (area between the shoulder blades)

When experiencing pain in the upper back, work the ball in between the shoulder blade and spine, gently roll against the wall in any direction. Be careful and do not press directly against the spine. If you curl your shoulder blades forward, you will better expose the rhomboid and slightly stretch them while you are working on them.

Note: Placing the tennis ball into a sock or pillowcase will help reduce the risk to dropping the ball and having to chase it. The pillowcase is not being shown, so that a better view of the placement of the ball is achieved.

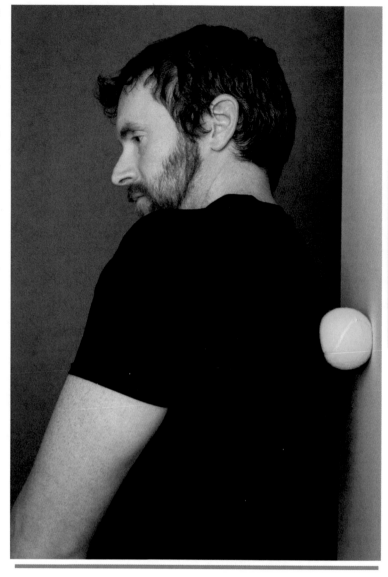

Figure 29: Tennis ball to the area between the shoulder blades, play with the angle for the best pressure

Rotator cuff (Infraspinatous, Teres Minor)

For problems and pain in the shoulder, working the area over top of the shoulder blade is almost always a must. There are four muscles of the rotator cuff all together; Two of them are not easily accessible and will therefore not be discussed. Located here are two of the two rotator cuff muscles that are more easily accessible and are used on a regular basis, partially due to poor posture. These two muscles respond very well to manual release.

When positioning yourself against the wall, you will have to slightly turn the body to the side that you are working on. If you stay flat against the wall, the ball will pop out the side since most of our bodies are curved. As you work through here you will potentially feel

Figure 30: Tennis ball, placed on the shoulder blade, keep turning the body to appropriately apply pressure. Note how the subject is turned slightly to the left to keep the ball flush against the wall

sensation down the arm, this is most likely muscular referral and not nerve related. Just make sure you are not pushing too hard and you will be fine. Remember though, I said sensation, not pain. Listen to your body as to what you are actually feeling. A pillowcase or sock holding the ball will make your life easier and reduce the risk of you dropping the ball.

Reminder:

You can perform self massage on any day; before, during, or after a workout, or just at any random time for fun. To maximize effectiveness, try massaging an area daily until you start to have trouble finding the areas of tightness (this can take up to a few weeks depending on how angry the area is).

Regardless of when you massage yourself, IT MUST FEEL GOOD!!!

2.3.4 Latissimus Dorsi (Lats)

The Lats are a huge and powerful muscle that start at the inside of the shoulder and wrap around to the low back. Since muscles of the body tend to be layered, you will also be hitting some of the other muscles close into the spine (more on that later). There are not really any precautions, other than just be careful around the shoulder itself.

There are multiple choices here. You can either go with the tennis ball against the wall or the foam roller on the floor. Either one works well. Each one just applies pressure a little differently.

Figure 31: Starting near the shoulder rolling towards the spine and down the back

The tennis ball does some nice work to the areas around the rib cage. There is not a specific motion that needs to be used here as there are multiple muscles that align in several directions. Feel free to roll side to side, up/down, or move in circular patterns. Just be careful and do not press directly onto the spine itself as you move closer to the midline of the body. This is to be only used while standing. The ribs will not like you laying on them when there is a ball placed between them and the ground (I can attest to this from personal experience, just do not do it).

Figure 32: Tennis ball to get the lower portion of the lats

With the foam roller start either in the low back and roll up towards shoulder, or at the shoulder and roll down towards the low back. You can basically massage the same areas as before using either an up and down motion or picking a specific spot and rocking the body side to side over the rib cage.

Figure 33-35: Using the foam roller, start near the shoulder and rolling towards the ribs as seen in the Top Left picture. Transition to upper back leaning more toward the same side as seen in the Middle figure. Finish farther down the back on the one side as seen in the Bottom Right figure. Repeat on the other side.

Special Note:

Remember to drink water. First of all, hydration is important in general. Second after you have massaged an area, extra water will help to flush the body of waste products that may have been trapped in tight areas. If your urine looks like apple juice, you may want to consider drinking more water. Please consult your doctor if you are unsure about your current level of hydration.

2.3.5 Deltoid

One of the pain movers of the arm, the deltoid is broken into three main areas pictured below. To hit the appropriate areas, gently roll against the wall. The half tennis ball works better than the full ball as it has less of a chance to fall, but you will not be able to move as much since the half-cut ball does not roll. These muscles have a tendency to be more sensitive than you realize, so start gently. While against the wall, keeping the hand next to the ball will help reduce the risk of the ball falling away and you accidently hitting the wall when it disappears suddenly.

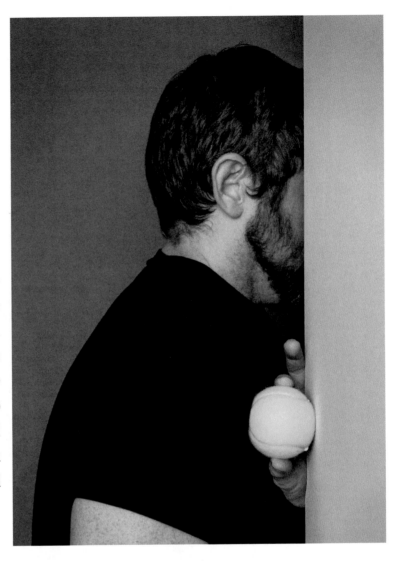

Figure 36: Tennis ball, anterior deltoid, the front of the shoulder itself. Keeping the hand in place to help prevent the ball from rolling away.

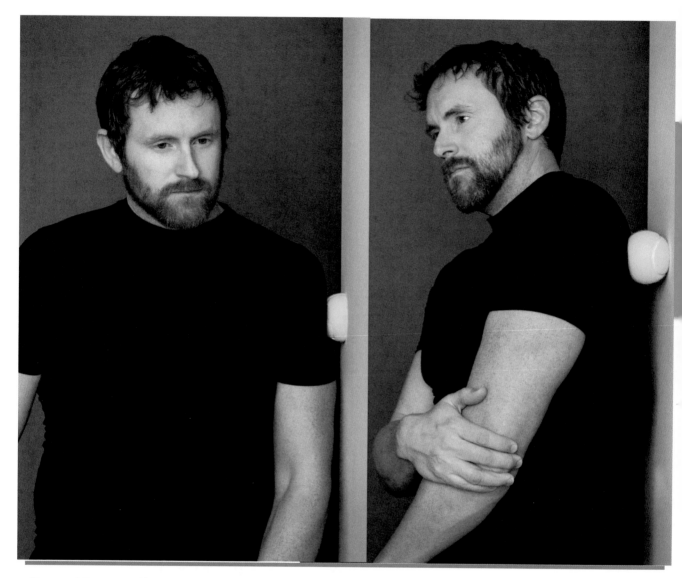

Figure 37-38: Half-cut tennis ball shown on the Left figure massaging the middle deltoid. Full tennis ball shown on the Right taking care of the posterior deltoid, the back of the shoulder itself

2.4 ARM

2.4.1 Triceps

Located at the back of the upper arm, the triceps does a good deal of pushing throughout the day. There are not many issues to be careful of other than as you get too close to the elbow and do not go into the armpit. You can get away with either the foam roller or the tennis ball for this area. I tend to recommend the roller unless you have really big triceps. You can also try a half-cut tennis ball in the area, which will tend not roll away from you.

The foam roller is by far the easiest of the options, just roll up/down or rock side to side and you will feel the work being done. The straighter or more bent the arm, the different the sensation. As the name will indicate to you, there are 3 sections to this muscle. Make sure you use different angles to get each portion.

Figure 39: Foam roller to the triceps as seen in the Left figure. In the figure on the Right, foam roller to the triceps with over pressure

The tennis ball is a viable option. Same basic idea as with the foam roller, just be careful the ball will try to escape. You can see the ball will not escape as easily if you brace the ball with your other hand or if you use a half-cut tennis ball.

Figure 41: Full tennis ball, using the other hand to help hold the ball in place

2.4.2 Bicep

The bicep does quite a bit of work, but it is not easy to use any of the tool mentioned earlier. It is really awkward to get the bicep other than just using your other hand (or convince someone else to help). The only real variation is to either press with the fingertips or to use your knuckles. If you put the arm against a chair or ball you can relax a little more as you apply pressure with the other hand.

Figure 42-43: Seen on the Top Left, using your fingertips to release the bicep. On the Bottom Right, using your knuckles to release the bicep

2.4.3 Forearm

The forearm is where most of the muscles are that control the hand/wrist. If you feel that the hands are tight or that you cannot squeeze as hard as you once used to be able to, work on the forearms to loosen the hands up.

As always stay away from the bonier parts of the arm. As you get close to the elbow itself, the ulnar nerve is close to the surface. If you feel tingling in your ring or little finger definitely stop pushing as you are pressing on the nerve. The same is true as you close in on the wrist. The median and ulnar nerves can potentially be compressed as you approach the bend/fold of the wrist; resulting in tingling of the palm side of the hand.

Also, as you approach the wrist, most of the surface muscles have changed into their corresponding tendons. Underneath these tendons there is one deeper muscle (pronator quadratus). Be careful trying to hit this muscle as you do not want to aggravate the aforementioned tendons. In addition to the nerves and tendons near the wrist, there are also blood vessels (both deep and shallow) as you may see them passing into the hand.

This is where a half-cut tennis ball becomes very useful. The forearm, for the most part, tends to be much more angular and allows a full-size ball to roll away. The use of a cylinder can be effective for a gentler massage, but tends to be rather ineffective for most. It just does not penetrate deep enough.

Place the half-cut ball on a firm surface cut side down. Place your forearm on top of the ball and gently rock over top of it in a side/side, forward/back, or circular pattern. For extra pressure you may place your other hand on top. The main bulk of the muscles you want to hit are located in the first half of the forearm, closer to the elbow.

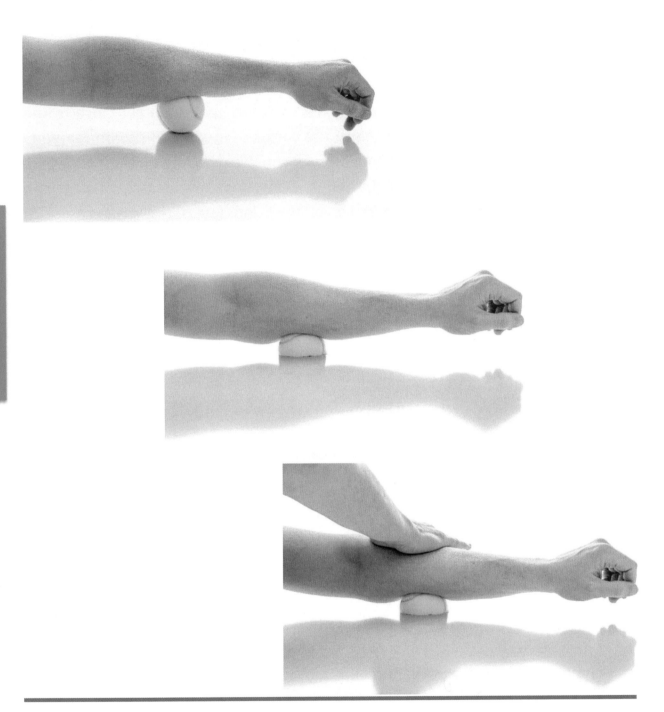

Figure 44-46: On the Top Left figure, full tennis ball used on the finger/wrist flexor. Middle figure has the half-cut tennis ball to the finger/wrist flexor. Bottom Right figure shows half-cut tennis ball with extra pressure

For the backside of the forearm, place the arm on a firm/supported surface, while you gently work the ball back and forth with the other hand. There are not as many precautions in this area as with the front side of the forearm. Basically just listen to the body. Either the full tennis ball or half-cut one work well here.

Figure 47-48: Top figure shows the full tennis ball to the finger/wrist extensors. Bottom figure uses the half-cut tennis ball to the finger/wrist extensors

2.4.4 Hand

This is pretty straightforward, your hand does everything for you, give it some love. Place a ball on a firm surface, then place a hand on top of it. You can use the other hand over top of the one you are treating will give some extra "oomph" to these small muscles. The half-cut tennis ball allows for more pressure to be applied due to the ball not rolling away, while the full tennis ball allows for more motion and freedom at the cost of pressure/control. Make sure you get the whole palm, especially near the thumb, it does quite a bit of work. Going with the golf ball instead of the tennis ball will get you a deeper pressure.

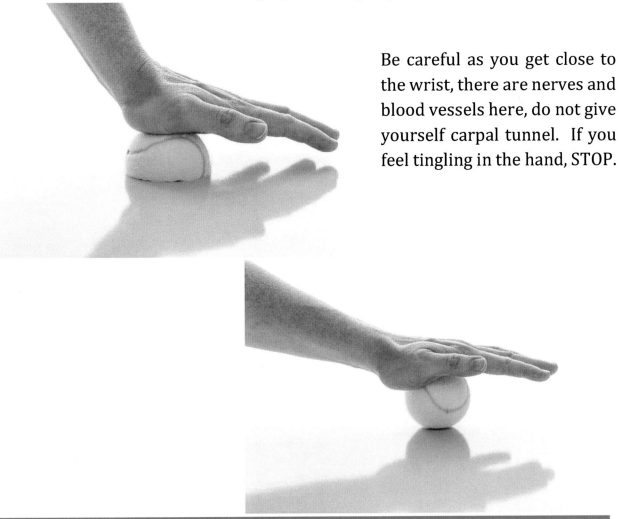

Be careful as you get close to the wrist, there are nerves and blood vessels here, do not give yourself carpal tunnel. If you feel tingling in the hand, STOP.

Figure 49-50: Top figure demonstrates half-cut tennis ball, for easier control, more pressure while the Bottom figure uses the full tennis ball, for more motion, less pressure

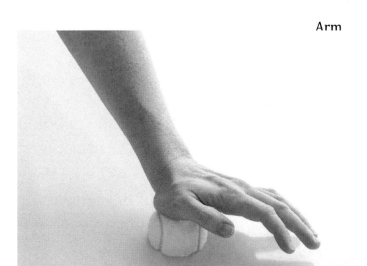

There are not any muscles in the fingers themselves, so keep to the palm to get the work done. There are not any muscles on the backside of the hand either, so do not worry about flipping your hand palm up (it would just be an awkward position anyway).

Figure 51-52: Top figure shows half-cut ball to the thumb side of the palm. Bottom figure uses the tennis ball adding an extra hand for more pressure.

There are muscles in between the bones of the hand (the interossei). They can be a challenge to hit as you need something smaller to use to massage or use your other hand. The easier way to find and work on them is to start with the palm on a firm surface. Place your finger from your other hand between the knuckles and move about 1 centimeter closer to the wrist. You are now between the metacarpals (the long bones of the hand) and you may feel the muscle here. For the most part, I would recommend an up and down motions (from the knuckles to the wrist) rather than a side to side motion due to the size of the area.

2.5 TRUNK

2.5.1 Thoracic Spine

The upper back/thoracic spine tends to be very tight due to poor posture and under use. Many of us cannot even engage the muscles properly here and tend to overuse the shoulder and lower back instead. Sitting at computers and using handheld devices can have us sitting with our heads forward or bent down too far placing an extra load on the upper back. When foam rolling this area it is not uncommon to hear some popping/creaking from the back; any noise that you happen to hear should not be accompanied by pain. Popping should be associated with relief or feeling lighter.

The foam roller can be less aggressive and you can get some nice stretching and loosening of the thoracic vertebrae. Just make sure that you support your head properly so that you do not create new traumas to have to work on. Remember you are cradling your head, not pulling on it.

Note: when you have your elbow out to the side, your shoulder blades will block the amount of stretch and work you get to the spine itself. When you bring your elbows in closer you will open up the space allowing better access to the spine.

To use the foam roller you have 2 main options. One is that you roll yourself up and down on the roller, going from the bottom of the rib cage to the top of the shoulder blades; you will have to lift your hips off of the ground to be able to roll up and down. Be careful not to get into the low back or hit the neck. Option two you will stop on an area in the upper back and gently relax backward over the roller; come back up then move to another area and repeat the relaxing over the roller.

Figure 53-55: Foam roller: in the Top Left figure we see the elbow relaxed out, working lower portion of thoracic region; the Middle figure shows elbows relaxed out, working on the upper portion of the thoracic region; The Bottom figure shows the elbows tucked in to expose more of the muscles of the spine

You can also lie on the foam roller length wise, keeping the head supported. Gently rock side to side for another potential release of the muscles next to the spine but maintain a small motion to be effective.

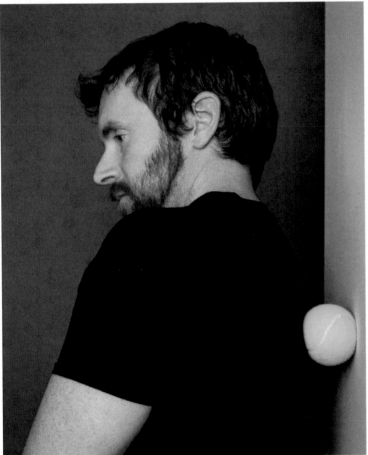

A tennis ball can be used to loosen up the muscles close into the back. Stay in close to the spine and work your way up and down, slightly side to side, or small circles close into the spine. (Tennis ball in a pillowcase makes it easier to use without dropping)

Figure 56-57: Top figure shows the foam roller, rocking side to side, small gentle motion. Bottom roller utilizes the tennis ball from the base of the neck to the low back to hit the muscles next to thoracic spine

2.5.2 Abdominals/Obliques

It is hard to work on the abdominals due to the lack of bony backing. Laying over the roller is the only way this works, and it is more of a stretch than a true release. Please be careful if you decide to work this tissue, remember that there are multiple organs sitting under these muscles (intestines, stomach, liver, spleen...) that really do not want to be squished aggressively. Please do not be overly aggressive. Remember what I had said a while ago "IF IT JUST HURTS, DON'T DO IT."

Gently lay over the roller. When you feel that a spot is sufficiently released, move to another spot. Do not roll around with this area, the organs will likely not

appreciate it. I generally do not recommend using a tennis ball here as there is not sufficient control or angle to be able to maneuver the ball, plus it is too small to work effectively. Be careful of the ribs, especially the lower ones as you are lying on your side.

Figure 58-59: With the foam roller in figure 58, the rectus abdominis is targeted just by lay on your stomach. Figure 59 shows the subject working on the obliques. Leaning slightly on the side/stomach to hit them

2.5.3 Low back

I only recommend using the tennis ball to the lower back as the foam roller is too aggressive to be used around the lower spine. The only exception to this is that if you wish to try and massage the quadratus lumborum (QL) which is talked about in the next section.

Figure 60: Tennis ball to the low back.

There is not much to it. Lean against the wall and roll away. Just do not push directly against the spine itself. There are plenty of small muscles close into the spine that will enjoy this process. If you bump against the bone, not a big deal, just do not try and push too hard which will aggravate the spine. Remember you are working on the muscles not the bones. As you move farther out to the sides away from the spine, the tennis ball will become less effective due to the lack of a firm backing to push the muscle against.

As can be seen in figure 60, the subject is turned more to the right than would be appropriate to maximize the angle of pressure, but he has turned to the right to help with visualization of the ball. You want to apply pressure towards the spine.

When using the foam roller to the low back, please use extreme caution… Or just do not do it. The spine at this level does not appreciate the abuse. (go to the QL section next for details or how to work the muscles adjacent low back).

Figure 61: Foam roller to the low back, it can be done, but should it?

2.5.4 QL

An awkward muscle to hit the Quadratus Lumborum (QL) is one that can help loosen and relieve the low back of tightness. It is a hard muscle to hit because you are not able to press directly in toward the body because of a lack of bony backing. The only substantial firm backing is the spine which can be used as discussed below.

The Thera Cane® tends to be the best tool to be used here. Wrap the Thera Cane® around the body as shown in the figures below (62, 63, 64). To find the QL, start at the spine, and then apply a gentle pressure/pull forward on the Thera Cane®. Keep the gentle pull as you slide the Thera Cane® out to the side of the body. Once the Thera Cane® shifts forward into softer tissue (about a third to halfway between the spine and side of the body) you will have just moved off the QL. Keep that gentle forward while you then press the Thera Cane® back into the direction of the spine

Figure 62: Thera Cane® to the QL, view of hand position

with the outer forearm which will then press the QL into the spine (remember bony backings make for better massage). Be gentle in this area, it takes a minute of finessing to be able to get the technique correct.

Figure 63-64: The figure on the Top Left using the Thera Cane® on the QL, side view of applied pressure in a forward/sideways manner, pressing toward the spine. The Bottom Right picture uses the Thera Cane® to the QL as seen from back

A foam roller can be attempted to release the QL, but it is not quite as effective. Lying on your side, place the foam roller in the empty space between the ribs and the pelvis. You will gently rock side to side over the roller as there is generally not much room here to roll on the roller up and down.

Figure 65: Foam roller to the QL

2.6 Hips

2.6.1 Hip Flexor

The hip flexor needs to be worked on. Because we all tend to sit too much (it starts in kindergarten), these muscles can become very tight. Extra tightness here can pull at the back, impair extension of the hip, and cause impaired gluteus maximus utilization.

However, this area generally responds much better to someone else doing the massaging as there is a much larger margin for error. There are three muscles that actually help to flex the hip. One is located in the quadricep muscle group, talked about in a later section. The second is the iliacus, which we can somewhat work on. And the third is the psoas which I would not recommend working on yourself at all. Have a professional work on the psoas for you as they will be more trained to apply the appropriate forces since the muscle is situated along the front/side of the lumbar spine (there are way too many organs in the way to reaching the psoas safely on your own).

The iliacus is the one that we will talk about. It is situated along the inside of the pelvic crest (the ilium). To start with, it is easiest to hit the muscle while laying or sitting reclined. To be able to massage it you will find the boniest section on the front of your pelvis (the ASIS) and move just to the inside of it. You will then angle a dull and smooth object, such as the end of a spoon, to a 30-45 degree angle and apply a gentle pressure toward the inside of the pelvis. DO NOT PRESS STRAIGHT BACK TOWARDS THE BACK OF THE BODY, there are organs here that you do not want to press on! You can work slightly higher and lower than this point, but always make sure that you are putting pressure towards the pelvis (30-45 deg). If you are unsure of how to achieve this, ask someone else to help explain, or just do not do it. You can always stretch this area as it generally likes a good stretch.

Figure 66-67: DO NOT GO STRAIGHT IN, there are organs. The figure on the Bottom Right shows the proper technique using the RangeRoller™ to work the iliacus. You must go in at an angle to be effective, push towards the pelvis

2.6.2 Gluteus Maximus/Piriformis

This area is a must. If it is functioning as normal, your gluteus maximus (here after referred to as simply the glut max) does a considerable amount of work throughout day. If it merely is acting as a cushion to sit on, please see your local physical therapist in order to relearn how to use this vital muscle.

Note: when the glut max is not working properly the hamstring and the low back muscles work harder than they are supposed to, so please relearn how to use the gluts.

Since this is a larger muscle you can either use the foam roller or tennis ball to release the tissue. The tennis ball does get in deeper than the roller due to its size. I recommend only using the tennis ball against the wall. I feel that using a ball on the floor is overly aggressive making it hard to relax and adjust the pressure being applied. However, if you decide to go this route, PLEASE make sure that you are relaxing and not causing pain.

Note: if you happen to feel any zing or other sensation down the leg, you may have hit the sciatic nerve. If you get this stop and re-adjust how you are applying pressure. Remember we are working on muscles not nerves here.

While laying on the roller, there is not a great deal of up and down motion to be had as the region is smaller. More of a leaning/rocking side to side over the roller will be used. Crossing the leg will amplify the sensation (as seen in figure 69).

Figure 68-69: Foam roller used in the Top figure is treating to the glut max (more gentle). The figure on the Bottom shows the foam roller to the glut max, stretch applied for varied sensation (generally more aggressive)

Gently lean against the wall and roll either side to side, up and down, or circular. The more that you manage to unload the weight from the leg you are working on, the more effective that the massaging will be. The closer the opposite leg is to the wall the less pressure that will be applied, and the farther away it is place the more pressure that will be applied.

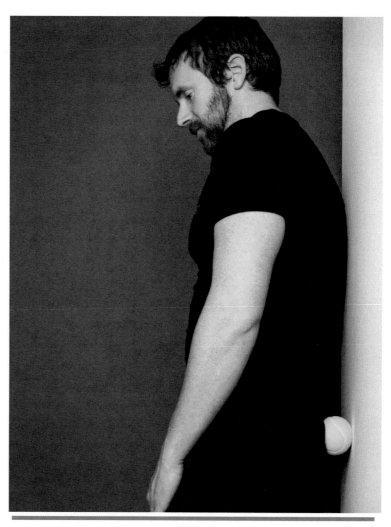

Figure 70: Tennis ball into the glut (varied pressure depending on opposite foot placement). The subject turned slightly away in order to better view the ball, for deeper penetration, he should be turned more to the left for actual self treatment

Gluteus Medius/TFL (Tensor Fasciae Latae)

This group of small muscles on the side of the hip are vital to supporting/stabilize the body on the standing leg. Any of the muscles on the side of the leg are a must to release as they also greatly affect rotational abilities. Using the wall is the most appropriate way to release this tissue as laying on the ground proves a great challenge to pressure modulation and relaxation on the ball. Remember if you need more pressure while leaning against the wall move your outer foot farther from the wall as you relax the leg you are working on. Unfortunately, there is not a picture for this area as it did not translate well visually as the other pictures had.

To find the gluteus medius, place a finger at the top of the pelvis and place the ball just below that finger. As I said above this is a small area to hit, so a forward and backward motion is more appropriate. Below this muscle you will find a bony prominence call the greater trochanter (it is the side of the hip bone). To aid in finding this bone it is generally the widest part of the hips. The reason you must be careful and not press on it as there is a bursae here and repeatedly rolling over it could cause bursitis.

The TFL will be in front of the gluteus medius as you move forward toward the front of the pelvis (the ASIS or the most bony front of the pelvis).

2.7 LEGS

2.7.1 Quadricep/IT band

The quadricep consists of four muscles all together. Three of these muscles control only the knee, while the most outer (rectus femoris) also assists with lifting/flexing the hip. It is common to see people rolling the outer thigh thinking they are addressing issues in their IT band, loosening it up. However, this is generally not the case since the trouble does not usually derive from the IT but rather the vastus lateralis (outer part of the quad/thigh) which is located underneath the IT band and beyond. There are cases where the IT band can truly be the culprit, but I would advise getting it looked at to appropriately treat it rather than trying to roll it out alone. Remember if you clench your teeth lighten up.

If your quadricep is very tight and tender start with a sitting position and a handheld device. Apply pressure gently at first then progressively apply more pressure. Start with an up and down motion. You can easily move at an angle or hold the roller in place while rocking it side to side over a particularly tight spot. Feel free to go all the way up toward the pelvis, but avoid hitting the knee at the other end.

Figure 71-72: RangeRoller™, In the figure on the Top Left having the foot more forward and relaxing the thigh will allow for a gentler massage. Using the RangeRoller™ in the Bottom Right bending the knee back will put a little more stretch on the quad as you massage

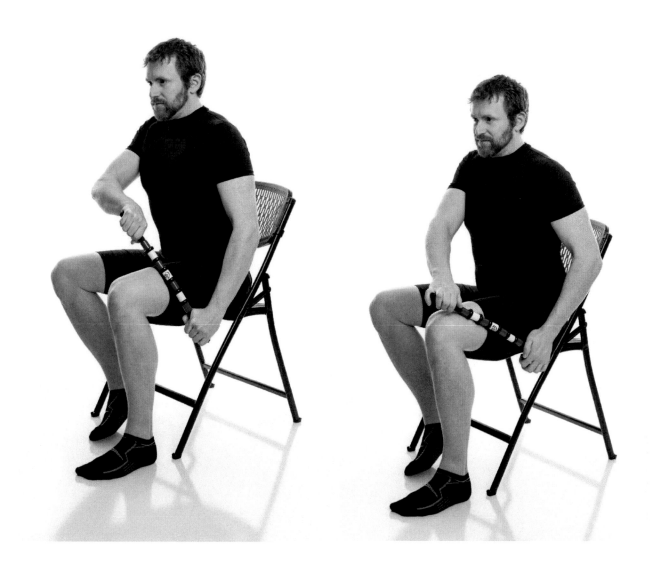

Figure 73-74: RangeRoller™. Do not just roll the top, tilt to the side to roll the outer portion of the quad as well. The figure on the Right using the RangeRoller™, keep trying different angles

Figure 75: RangeRoller™, This is not directly on the inner thigh, stay positioned top/inside region of the quad

When you are ready for more pressure and the hand roller does not cut it anymore but you know that you are still tight, we move to the floor. Using the arms and one of the legs to control the motions over top of the roller. To take even more pressure off you could even put the toe down for the leg that you are rolling. Same principles apply when rolling forward and back over top of the roller or rocking side to side over more key spots. For more pressure you remove points of contact with the ground, until you eventually are only on the forearms and one leg is stacked on top of the other.

Figure 76-78: Foam, Top Left figure is with a single leg (most gentle); Top Right figure is both legs at once (medium pressure); Bottom figure is stacked legs (most aggressive)

Note: After you have stacked the legs, you may feel as though you are not getting deep enough, ask yourself if you are truly relaxing the thigh or if you have tightened up again. If you are relaxed, then the muscle is likely fine, so stop rolling on it.

For the vastus lateralis and IT band use the same tech as above, but on the side of the thigh. Be careful about going too high up the leg and hitting the outer part of the hip bone (greater trochanter). There is a bursae here which will not want to be hit/rolled over, if you are unsure of where this is, it is located at the widest part of the hips below the pelvis. If you place your hand on the side of your hip and rotate your leg back and forth you should feel the bone move.

Figure 79-80: Top Left figure with foam to the ITB and outer quad, other leg providing support (more gentle). Bottom Right using foam to the ITB and outer quad with legs stacked (more intense)

2.7.2 Adductors

The inner thigh is another area that tends to be tight for many people. There are several muscles that make up the adductor group. At times when the inside of the knee may be bothering you (medial side), there is a good chance that the adductors are too tight and pulling on the knee causing your pain.

NOTE: if you feel a pulsing while pressing or rolling over an area, that would be your pulse. Move the pressure to a nearby area so that you do not cut off the blood flow to the lower leg.

To reach the adductors gently roll on the inner thigh. As seen in figure 81, the body is mostly supported by the ground so less pressure will be placed onto the roller. You can move the body forward and back rolling along the foam or rock gently up and down vertically along the stationary roller keeping the leg relaxed. Be careful and do not hit the knee itself. For more pressure, reposition the body more on top of the roller as seen in figure 82.

Figure 81-82: Foam roller being used in the figure on the Top Left with body on ground (more gentle). Figure on the Bottom Right uses foam roller with more body weight on the roller

For a more gentle massage opt for a hand roller. Sit forward near the edge of a chair to allow for easier access. Gently roll up and down the thigh. Once you find a good spot feel free to rock back and forth. Make sure you do not hit the knee, it will not appreciate it.

Figure 72: RangeRoller™, for the adductor (most gentle)

2.7.3 Hamstring

The hamstring is comprised of 3 muscles. They have a huge impact on both the knee and the hip as each of the muscles attaches above and below the thigh bone (femur). This means that they have the potential to move the one or both joints while the muscles activate. I have found that using the foam roller is not as effective as the spherical object. Laying down can be effective when the hamstrings are more sensitive, but if you need a deeper penetration, you will want to sit for this one.

While using the foam roller you can move forward and back, or gently rock side to side. You can stack the legs here to make it more intense or keep the legs next to each other for a more gentle sensation.

Figure 64: Foam roller to the hamstrings

To use the tennis ball, sit on a firm surface, such as a chair. This is generally the most effective way to release the hamstring. Place the ball under the thigh and gently move the thigh side to side. Trying to shift the body forward and back is just awkward, plus the way the fibers of the hamstring are lined up, it is just more effective to massage them while moving side to side. Make sure that you do not just get the middle of the thigh, also work out towards the sides.

Once you have cleared an area, move closer to the knee or the hip. Do not stay on one spot more than 90 seconds. The points to be careful of here are staying about 2 finger widths away from the knee,

Figure 85: Be careful as you approach the knee, do not get too close

as well as staying about 2 fingers widths away from the bones that you sit on (ischial tuberosity if you want to be technical).

If the chair that you are sitting on is too soft, place a magazine on the cushion, the ball on top of the magazine, then your leg on top of the ball. The magazine will allow for more pressure to be applied as it does not allow the ball to sink into the cushion as deeply. If there is too much pressure being applied by the ball you can place items under the foot, which will lift the thigh higher off of the ball as seen in figure 86.

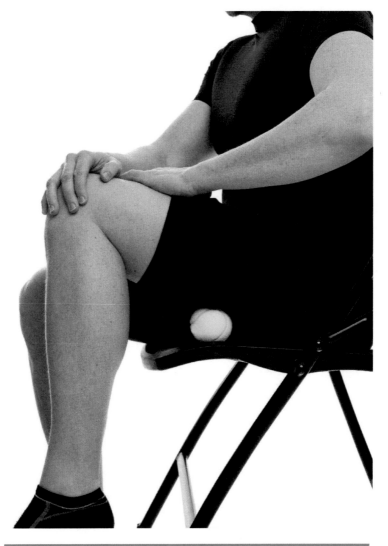

Figure 86: You can always place something under the foot in order to raise the leg higher and reduce the pressure

To use the hand roller, position yourself comfortably on the ground or the edge of a chair while you move the roller back and forth across the back of the thigh as seen in figure 87 and 88.

Figure 87-88: RangeRoller™, to the hamstring various angles

Reminder:

KEEP IT COMFORTABLE

(I told you I was going to keep reminding you)

2.7.4 Calf

The calf is another area that takes a large amount of abuse and not enough care. We tend to have a great deal of tightness in the calves, which can place an extra stress load on the surrounding joints of the foot, knee, and even having an impact on areas higher above. In general, the cylindrical objects do well here in loosening the area. There are more options for movement. If you do really need more pressure, then a sphere will work more aggressively. Make sure that you are actually relaxing the foot and ankle all the way. This will allow you deeper into the muscle.

Start with working the center of the calf. Forward and backward motions work well. After you have rolled forward and back several times, begin to start keying in on certain spots. Once you have located a more sensitive area, either use a very small motions forward and backward, stay stationary directly on it, or rock gently side to side. Then turn the leg slightly either inward and outward and repeat the process of moving forward and backward looking for further trigger points on the sides of the calf. Stacking the legs makes the process more aggressive. NOTE: Do NOT press directly behind the knee and be careful as you approach the heel.

Progression can be seen below in figures 89, 90, and 91; starting with the single leg and progressing towards the stacked legs with lifting the hips from the ground.

Figure 89-91: Top Left one leg (most gentle), Middle stacked legs (more intense), Bottom Right stacked legs and using arms to lift the hips from the ground (most intense)

In the figure to the left, the tennis ball can be seen. The tennis ball moves around quite a bit. A pillowcase of sock helps to significantly reduce the speed of rolling. For more pressure, careful stack the legs, but be aware that the ball has a greater tendency towards rolling out. Stacking is more appropriate when using the half-cut ball as it will not roll away and can provide a more intense

Figure 92: Tennis ball used on the calf

massaging sensation.

We will end with a hand roller. Use of the hand roller can be effective, but positionally, I feel that it is the most awkward and can potentially place too much stress on the low back, especially if you already have low back issues. This is, however, a good tool to try and convince someone else to use by pulling the hand roller up and down the calf rather than you trying to awkwardly reach it. You can just sit back and relax while they do the hard work.

Figure 93-94: RangeRoller™, side view on the left and angled view to the right

2.7.5 Foot

So we have finally come to the foot. Often it is neglected and under/improperly used, especially while it is stuffed inside a shoe all day long. The foot loves to be massaged. There are many nooks and crannies to be filled depending on the size of your arch. So we have several options here. The foot generally does well with spherical objects more than cylinders due to their ability to reach those tight spots. As always the tennis ball is the easy go to, but a golf ball can really shine here. If you are having any issues with true plantar fasciitis, then a frozen golf ball can be one of your best friends. The golf ball will not stay as cold as a frozen water bottle, but it can get into places that the water bottle is unable. At times I sometimes recommend using the water bottle first, more gently, then switching over to a golf ball for certain sections.

Figure 95: Tennis ball rolled in the arch

To work the foot, keep your tool on the ground while you gently roll your foot over top of it. If more pressure needs to be applied, just easily shift more weight onto it. Again placing the ball into a sock or pillow case will help to reduce the rolling speed giving you more control.

Work around the entire arch of the foot and out to the base of each of the toes. You may use any direction for the foot (forward/back, side to side, circles, or a combination).

There are really limited concerns when working in the foot. The only area that really stands out is being more careful around the bottom of the heel where the plantar fascia actually connects. As this area is not very muscular, you would be mostly working the tendons or other connective tissue and potentially aggravating it in the process.

A word of caution: it may be tempting to stand and roll the ball, if you decide that sitting really just does not get into the foot enough, please use caution it is easy to get carried away here. Especially with the golf ball.

Figure 96-97: Figure on the Top Right, be sure to roll the ball forward towards the toes. Figure on the Bottom Leg rolling the water bottle in the arch.

3 SECTION: BONUS MATERIAL

3.1 ADVANCED TECHNIQUE

Once you have become confident with being able to relax and massage an area, there is another technique that can be utilized in order to help the muscle to release. Looking once more at the pictures of the calf with the foot pulled toward you and away (figure 98), you noticed earlier in the previous pages that the calf sinks in while relaxed.

If you keep the foam roller focused on one spot while you pump the foot this will massage the calf differently and some would say more intensely. As you point the foot down, the roller will not sink in until you relax at the end of the downward motion and will stay relaxed momentarily as you start to pull the toes back toward you. This back and forth motion will help to release the muscle while it is actively being used.

Figure 98: Locking the calf onto one spot, gently pump the foot up and down for a different massaging sensation

This concept can be used with any of the muscles. Pin the muscle down with your tool of choice, then gently start moving the limb around. For instance, if you are using the tennis ball to the back of the shoulder against the wall, you can gently swing the arm around, reach over your head, or twist the arm back and forth. Listen to the body, it will tell you which motions are appropriate and which are too intense. NO PAIN, MORE GAIN!

Another example can be seen below for the adductor, figure 99. Lock the inner thigh into one place while you rotate the leg up and down.

And Lastly here is an example of moving while working on the jaw as seen in figure 100.

Figure 99: Rotate the leg up and down

Figure 100: Gently open and close the jaw while keeping the fingers in place on the masseter

3.2 CONCLUSION

Thank you for reading "The Art of the Self Massage." I hope that it has been informative and that you can use the knowledge within this book to start helping yourself to feel better and gain more control over your body.

If you found this book to be helpful, please look out for my next book which will discuss fine tuning your muscles in order to give you better posture, more support, and proper muscular use. Many of us do not know how to use certain muscles correctly. By focusing on key areas you will have a chance to gain better building blocks to meet your goals, whether they are to lose weight, gains strength, or just have better awareness of your body.

4 ABOUT THE AUTHOR

Jason Cain has been a physical therapist practicing since 2006. He Graduated from Armstrong Atlantic State University with a Master of Physical Therapy, then from Medical College of Georgia with a Doctorate of Physical Therapy. His focus of treatment has been with outpatient orthopedics, covering all joints from head to foot. He has always had a passion for hands on work, but realized that the effects could be short lived and that if patients could have greater access to muscular release through massage they would have better outcomes. Over the years he has focused on educating patients on how to perform self massage to various body parts and decided to condense that education down into a book. When not working he enjoys being physically active and spending time with family and friends.

Please feel free to contact me with any questions: jcain.pt@gmail.com

Made in the USA
Middletown, DE
02 September 2019